Colores de la vida

Mexican Folk Art Colors in English and Spanish

Cynthia Weill

Folk Art by Artisans from Oaxaca

RED

* * * * *

ROJO

Yellow

* * * * * * *

Amarillo

Blue

* * * * * * *

Azul

GREEN

❋ ❋ ❋ ❋ ❋

VERDE

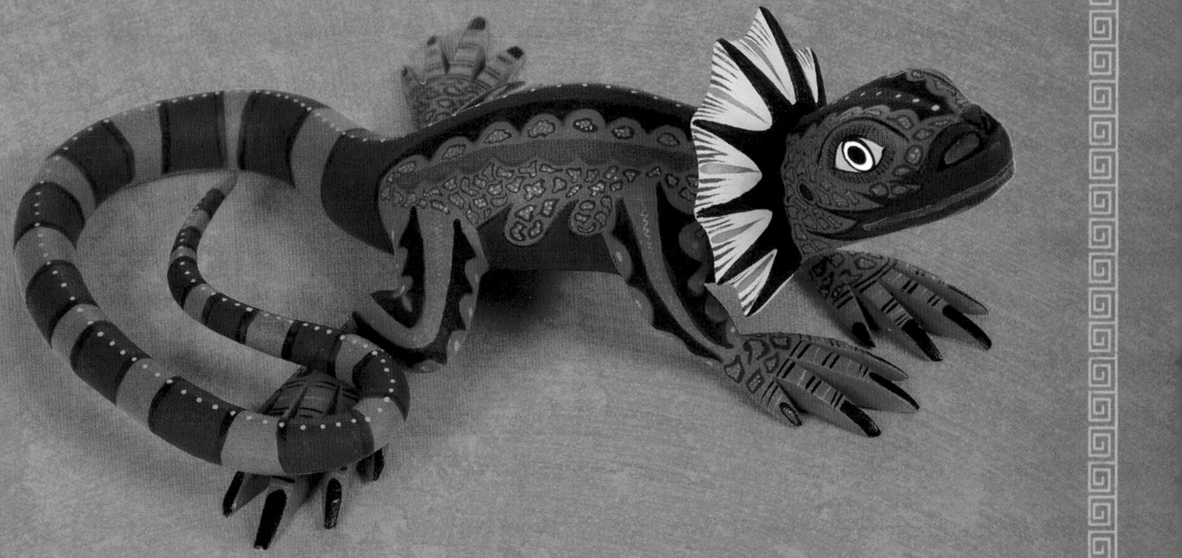

Orange

Anaranjado

PINK

* * * * * *

ROSA

PURPLE

✻ ✻ ✻ ✻ ✻

MORADO

TURQUOISE

* * * * * *

TURQUESA

BROWN

❋ ❋ ❋ ❋ ❋

CAFÉ

Black

✿ ✿ ✿ ✿ ✿

Negro

WHITE

❋ ❋ ❋ ❋ ❋ ❋

BLANCO

GRAY

❋ ❋ ❋ ❋ ❋ ❋ ❋

GRIS

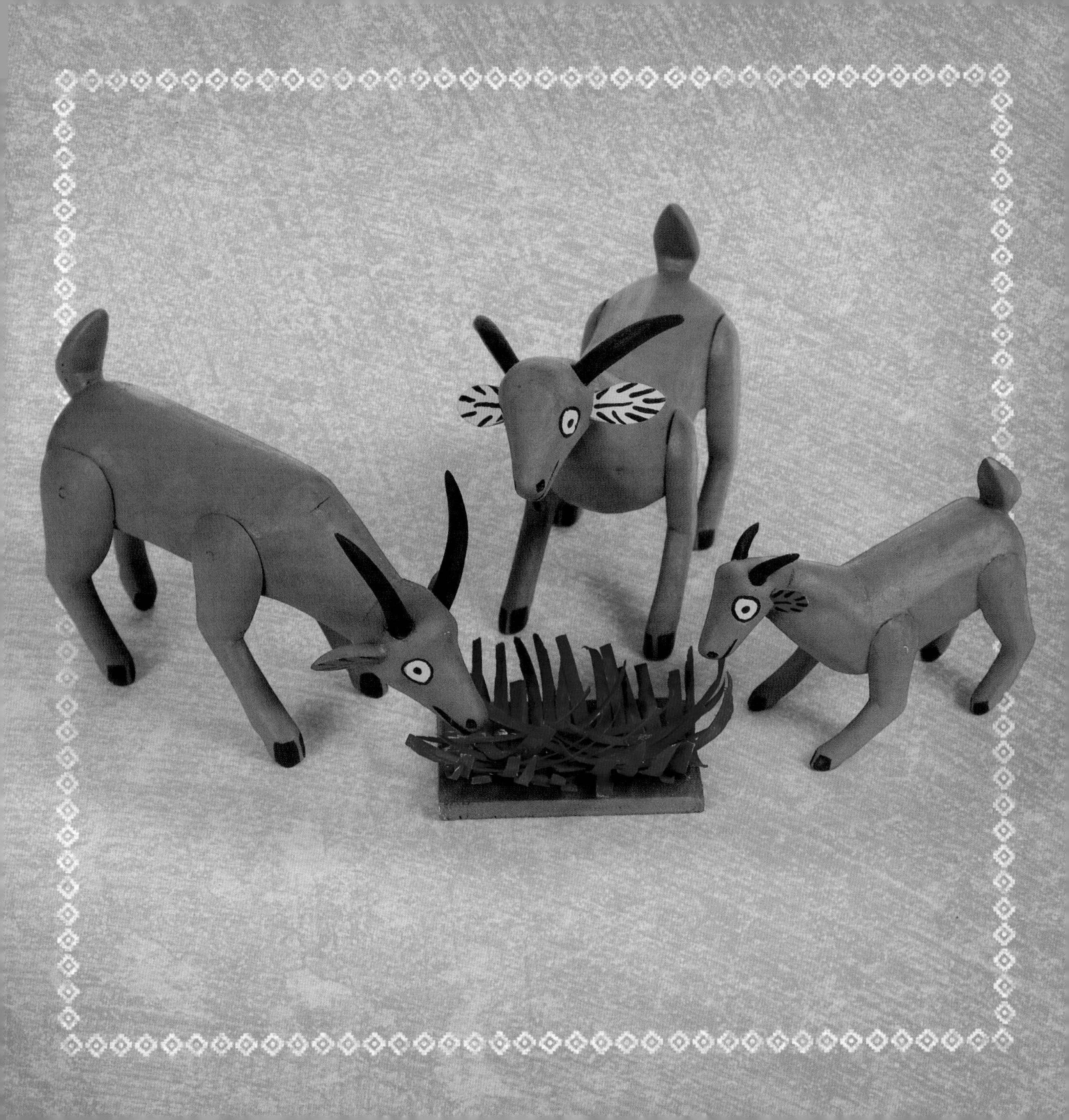

GOLD

�֍ �֍ ✤ ✤ ✤ ✤ ✤

DORADO

SILVER

* * * * * *

PLATEADO

Can you say all
the colors in Spanish?

❋ ❋ ❋ ❋ ❋

¿Puedes nombrar todos
los colores en inglés?

Home of woodcarver Julio Jiménez, La Unión

Dedication

To: Bruce, Vicky, Bryant, Alexander, Nicholas and Mom: You are the colors of my life!

Photographs by

Otto Piron

Thanks to

Jaime Ruiz, Friends of Oaxacan Folk Art, José Miguel Moracho, Kirsten Darling, Janet Glass,
Ruth Borgman, Myriam Chapman, Jan Asikainen, Jorge Luis Santiago, Casa Colonial in Oaxaca, Mexico.

The artisans represented in *Colores de la vida* are:

From San Martín Tilcajete
Piggies: Maria Jiménez
Cat: Jesús Sosa/Juana Vicente
Lion: Rubí Fuentes/Efraín Broa
From Oaxaca City
Fish, Chickens: Miguel Ángel Agüero
Dragon babies: Pedro Mendoza

From La Unión
Goats, Rabbits, Cows: Eloy Santiago
From San Bártolo Coyotepec
Spider: Carlomagno Pedro Martínez

Sun: Apolinar Aguilar

From Arrazola
Possums: Moisés Jiménez
Lizard: Mario Castellanos
Polar Bears: Eleazar Morales
Giraffes: René Mandarín

Musicians: Angélica Vásquez

Cover and Book Design by

Sergio A. Gómez

FIRST EDITION   10 9 8 7 6 5 4 3 2 1
Weill, Cynthia. Colores de la vida : Mexican folk art colors in English and Spanish : folk art by artisans from Oaxaca / by Cynthia Weill. -- 1st ed. p. cm. -- (First concepts in Mexican folk art series ; 3) English and Spanish. ISBN 978-1-933693-82-8 (alk. paper) 1. Folk art--Mexico--Oaxaca (State)--Juvenile literature. 2. Color in art--Juvenile literature. 3. Colors, Words for--Juvenile literature. I. Title. II. Title: Mexican folk art colors in English and Spanish. III. Title: Folk art by artists from Oaxaca. IV. Series. NK845.O2W454 2010 701'.85097274--dc22
 2010014669

CINCO PUNTOS PRESS

EL PASO, TEXAS